BANARAS

BANARAS

SACRED CITY OF INDIA

Introduction and 96 colour photographs by

RAGHUBIR SINGH

THAMES AND HUDSON

To Anne and Devika

First published in Great Britain in 1987 by
Thames and Hudson Ltd, London

Printed and bound in Switzerland

CONTENTS

Acknowledgments

*I would like to thank the following persons for their help and
encouragement in the making of this book:*

Maharaja of Banaras H.H. Vibhuti Narain Singh
Pundit Ravi Shankar
Dr Rai Anand Krishna
Mahendra Shah
Asha and Ketaki Sheth
Dr Bhanu Shankar Mehta
Mahant Vir Bhadra Mishra
Shri Raman
J.P. Gupta
R.P. Gupta
William Gedney
Dr P.N. Singh
Mrs N. Rajam
Mohan Hemadi
Naval Krishna
Kalyan Krishna
Ajit and Jane Cheema
Appan Menon
J.N. Supakar
Tarun Kumar Basu
Mahant Ram Shankar Tripathi

INTRODUCTION

In Rajasthan, my home state in north-western India, there is one perennial river. The Chambal tumbles all year round through a land of rock and shrub. The other rivers are parched and lifeless most of the year. It is in the monsoon that they flow furiously, sometimes washing away villages. As a child, I found the idea of a city set right on the banks of a fearsome river very strange. An ancient city whose life was intimately tied to the Ganges came alive in the tales my deeply religious mother told me, tales that she and the elders brought back from Banaras, which held me captive long before I ever saw the city. From then on, I was bewitched by the myth and mystery of Banaras.

It was fifteen years later that I first visited the city. I arrived during a solar eclipse. The crowds of bathers, the overloaded boats, the temples and palaces appeared for a minute or two to be painted in gold as the sun moved into an eclipse and the light changed from a late-morning glare to a rare Rembrandt-like luminescence. This memory of my first sight of the Banaras riverfront is still etched in my mind.

Equally vivid is my first brush with a Banarasi. Since then, the seamier side of the city and the pertinacity of the Banarasis have often bothered me, despite my frequent visits. Over the last twenty years I have developed a love-hate relationship with the people of Banaras.

The first Banarasi I ever met was a *panda* – the ritual specialist who waits to pounce on pilgrims. He was tall and slim in a white shirt and dhoti. Over his right shoulder was draped a *gamchha* (a scarf-cum-towel) – a ubiquitous piece of clothing in Banaras. He ran alongside my rickshaw as it wound its way to Dashaswamedh, the city's most sacred *ghat* or bathing steps. His manner clearly established that he was a veteran *panda*. Through persistent probing and practiced inquiry, he discovered that I was new to the city, that I knew no one and that I planned to stay for a week. At first I had innocently answered his endless questions but soon I realized that I had given away too much. In me, he saw a week's wages. Gingerly, I tried to shake him off. He threatened me with damnation, warning me that it was my duty as a Hindu to hire a Brahmin guide, or else I sinned. He finally gave up when I rented a boat and was rowed out onto the river.

Since then, I have had similarly unpleasant encounters with alarming regularity. It is common, for example, for even policemen to stop the three-wheeled motor taxis (called 'autos') and attempt to hijack them to a destination of their choice. I gradually grew adept at fighting off these guardians of the law. It was while I was perfecting my defensive techniques that I participated in two interesting nocturnal events.

Late one evening I was riding an auto to the river when a motor-bike with three riders roared up, braked and blocked the way. My driver stopped abruptly. The Banarasi who drove the vehicle commanded me to get out and asked his passengers, a couple – obviously his relatives – to get in. I refused and held up my tripod menacingly. I even threatened to take him to the police, but he would not budge from the motor-bike. At this point the couple intervened, imploring him to get a grip on himself – I think he was high on *bhang*, cannabis – and motioning me to carry on. Only then did my driver start nervously fidgeting with the ignition, and soon we were on our way. Above the putter of the engine rose a stream of unprintable expletives. I began to understand the saying that the first words a Banarasi child learns are curses.

The second experience was even more disagreeable. It began when I took a photograph of a shopkeeper at dusk. Seeing my flash go off, he charged out of his shop and demanded that I destroy the roll of film. When I refused, an altercation followed and a crowd gathered. There were sympathizers for both sides. In the midst of this, a man emerged who identified himself as the landlord of the building and stated that he had no objection to my photographing it. He led me aside and asked what had happened. Convinced that I was no threat, he made an unsuccessful attempt at appeasing the shopkeeper (his tenant). Finally, the only solution seemed to be to resolve things at the police station.

The Chowk police station is built like a medieval fortress with a massive gate. An inspector sat at a desk and other policemen lounged about. Each of us narrated our versions of the story. The landlord stood by my side and declared that he was willing to put it in writing that he had no objection to my photographing his building. Despite this, the police treated me as if I had committed a serious offence and threatened to confiscate my cameras. At this turn of events, the shopkeeper broke into idiomatic and sarcastic Hindi which is special to Banaras. He also laced his speech with quotations from the epic *Ramayana*, on which Banaras bases much of its morality. The police, now joined by their colleagues, had found their entertainment for the evening. The account was narrated again and again in different versions. I was accused of being stubborn, disrespectful and ignorant of the law and was detained for three exasperating hours. During this time I tried to telephone two officials I had previously met, but they were not at home. I finally gave up when one policeman flatly asked, 'If I ran naked through the street, could you take my photograph without my permission?' I surrendered my roll of film, took a receipt and left. I learned later that the shopkeeper suspected I was in league with the landlord, who had filed a suit against him. Tenant and landlord litigation and illegal occupancy lawsuits are common to Banaras.

The next morning I telephoned a senior official in Banaras. After he had heard me out, he commented: 'The police do not know the law. I will have your film returned to you in the hotel. Do not go to the police station.' Then he paused and asked, 'What are you doing this evening? Come and share a drop of liquor with me.' I accepted. That evening the civil servant told me: 'The law and order situation is bad, especially on the riverfront at night. It is unsafe. The area is run by murderers and thieves.'

As I learned more and more about the city's history, I took comfort in the fact that not only the average visitor, like myself, but also some of the more illustrious persons in Indian history have suffered at the hands of the Banarasis. Among those who were made unwelcome was the Buddha, who walked 200 miles on what 2,500 years later came to be known as the Grand Trunk Road. It ran from Gaya in Bihar State (where he gained enlightenment), to Sarnath near Banaras, where he preached his first sermon in the 6th century BC. It is significant that the Banarasis considered this new visionary to be a heretic and did not welcome him. Even today, though the Buddha is accepted in Hinduism as the ninth incarnation of the god Vishnu, there is no shrine or sanctuary to him within the city. Sarnath, with its Buddhist monuments, is four miles north of Banaras. 'The Hindi word *budhoo* (meaning idiot) is rooted in Banaras's first contemptuous assessment of the Buddha,' the scholar of Banarasi life Dr Bhanu Shankar Mehta told me.

Tulsi Das (1543–1623 AD), the poet who popularized the vernacular language of Hindi, lived and died in Banaras. He wrote a Hindi version of the *Ramayana*, which is the most popular religious literature in north and central India's vast Hindi-speaking belt. When Tulsi Das wrote his famous work, it was important for him to receive the blessings of the pundits of Banaras. But instead of blessing him, they were openly hostile because he had shunned classical Sanskrit. According to one story, the pundits attempted to ascertain the worth of the work by placing it overnight in the Vishwanath Temple, the city's most important place of worship. It was kept at the bottom of a pile of classical scriptures including the Vedas. By morning the Tulsi *Ramayana* had moved to the top of the stack.

In our own times, the film-maker Satyajit Ray's experience of the Banarasis is worth recalling. When Ray was shooting a day-for-night sequence for his film *Joi Baba Felunath* in Banaras, the filming attracted large crowds, who ignored a police plea for the deserted street that Ray needed. In utter frustration, the film-maker retreated to his hotel room, where he seriously contemplated rewriting that portion of the script. Just then, he was visited by a group of *goondas* (street toughs), the Banarasi variety of which are known for their deep pride in their city. They reassured him that they could organize a deserted street. Sure enough, the next day, when the film crew returned to the same street, not a soul was in sight.

From time to time, when the honour of the city has been at stake, the *goondas* of Banaras have risen to the occasion. Sometimes they have even played their part in the city's history. When Warren Hastings, the East India Company's first Governor-General, imprisoned Chet Singh, the ruler of Banaras, in 1781, in the latter's riverfront palace – for resisting the tax demands of the English – the raja escaped from the upper stories of the building by means of a rope improvised of turbans. He rallied a local rebellion composed of Banarasi *goondas*, a group which was powerful enough to make Hastings flee for his life.

The people of holy Banaras are masters at mixing the sacred with the profane, having had more than 2,500 years of practice since the city was founded in approximately 800 BC.

No one knows the precise date of the city's foundation, but Banaras is as old as Peking, Athens and Jerusalem. In one sense it is older, because it has an unbroken living tradition. In this respect it is the oldest city in the world. Through its continuous calendar it spans all the centuries of Indian civilization. Sensing this, Mark Twain, after a visit in 1896, wrote in *Following the Equator* (1897): 'Benares is older than history, older than tradition, older even than legend, and looks twice as old as all of them put together!'

At the northern edge of the city, overlooking the Ganges, is the Rajghat plateau, a place of partially excavated ruins. It is speculated that as early as the end of the second millennium BC this was an outpost of an Aryan tribe. The Aryans first worshipped the elements: the forests, the rivers, the sky, the earth, the air and fire. From this heritage Banaras came to be known at an early stage as the Forest of Bliss. The Aryan tribe was the Kashis and from them Banaras gets its other name – Kashi: 'the Luminous' or the 'the City of Light'. Modern India officially uses the name Varanasi, an ancient name found in the *Mahabharata* and the Buddhist Jataka tales. From the Pali version of Varanasi emerged the corrupted name: Banaras – the city's most popular name today. The Kashi kings probably participated in the great war immortalized in the epic *Mahabharata*. As Hinduism evolved, so did Banaras, until it became 'the chief city of all India'. In a religious sense it remains so today, drawing people from every corner of India. But the city we see today is physically less than 300 years old. Ancient and medieval Banaras, with all its monumental temples, was destroyed by waves of Moslem invaders. In 1194, when Qutb-ud-din Aibak, the Commander-in-Chief of Mohammed Ghuri, wreaked complete destruction, the city was shifted southwards to its present location on the vast bend of the Ganges, which flows south to north at Banaras. While Hinduism continued to resist and revive, Aibak's destruction was a death blow for the Buddhism of Banaras.

From Aryan times to Moghul times and from Moghul times to modern times, despite repeated ups and downs, this tenacious city has given itself a new lease of life. This is of course due to the nature of its people. In *Following the Equator* Mark Twain called Banaras a 'beehive of religion'. The worker bees: the priests, the *pandas*, the pilgrims, the dyers, the weavers, the sculptors, the silversmiths, the jewellers, the musicians, the holy men, the writers, the poets and so many others who make up Banaras hail from all parts of India. They have settled in Banaras through the ages, bringing with them customs, manners and names. They have even developed whole neighbourhoods which are characteristic to their origins. In view of this, one Baranasi, hailing from Gujarat State in Western India, told me, 'All Banarasis are outsiders,' though he and his family consider themselves quintessential Banarasis.

With this all-India assemblage of people in Banaras came the various gods of India, supposedly 330 million of them. But the presiding deity is Shiva, who guards and protects Banaras. Shiva emerged from the Vedic god Rudra. In the *Rig Veda* there are several hymns to Rudra-Shiva. Shiva the mountain god who dwelt at Kailas, the most sacred mountain for Hindus and Buddhists, came down to the Gangetic Plain to become a city-dwelling family man in the very heart of this city of culture: Banaras. Here death is not to be feared, for with Shiva himself as guru, Kashi has the power of bestowing liberation from the cycle of reincarnation not only on human beings but also on animals, birds and insects. Therefore thousands of Shaivite shrines dot Banaras but the most important place of worship, the Vishwanath Temple, is dedicated to Shiva as the Lord of All: Vishwanath. When Aurangzeb the Moghul Emperor ordered the destruction of three important temples and the building of mosques on their sites, in 1669, a priest salvaged the Vishwanath *lingam*, representing the divine energy of Shiva, and hid it. After the event a small shrine was erected where today's Vishwanath Temple stands. The Maharani Ahilya Bai of Indore, a devotee, built the present temple in 1777. The Sikh ruler Ranjit Singh gave a donation in 1839 to gild the roof of the temple.

On one visit to Banaras, in 1982, I arrived a day after the Vishwanath Temple had been robbed. In the night the thieves had made off with the ceremonial silver, the temple jewellery and the golden *yoni* – the representation of Parvati, the consort of Shiva. The black stone *lingam* remained. Because the police believed it was an inside job, the government moved quickly, taking away the management from the *mahants* – the high priests who had overseen the temple for a hundred years – and appointing instead a civil servant with an understanding of Hinduism.

Soon after my arrival, the new *yoni*, shaped like a golden disc, was installed. With hammers and chisels a group of goldsmiths added the last touches, watched by a crowd of protective policemen and bureaucrats. Then the *lingam* was washed in Ganges water. It was decorated with roses, marigolds, jasmine, Bengal quince leaves and sandalwood paste. Incense was lighted. Ganges water was poured in the square silver-lined pit housing the *yoni*. Vedic hymns were sung. Cymbals clashed, bells chimed and the beat of drums climaxed in a single unified rhythm. At that moment a priest bowed and offered *arati* (an invocation with sanctified fire) to Baba Vishwanath. This act invoked the deity. The sanctified fire, a lamp of many tiers with wicks in odd numbers, was carried through a crowd of worshippers to an adjacent building along with the ceremonial silver. The worshippers within reach extended their hands to the flames and then pulled them back to touch their heads with their fingertips. Simultaneously there were repeated shouts of *Bom, Bom, Bholey!* This is an unintelligible sound called *hudukkar* which a Shaivite yogi makes at one stage of worship. It pleases Shiva immensely. In spite of the frenzied crowd there were those on whose faces I could read deep inner tranquillity and satisfaction. I watched their faces change expression as they returned to earth. This was Kashi – the Luminous.

Banaras was alive again. The robbery had paralysed the city, but with the reopening of the temple and the arrest of a few underling priests, the worker bees of Banaras were bustling about and back in business.

The labyrinth of lanes throbbed with life. Standing outside the Vishwanath Temple I could see that the old lanes were built to provide security. From the exterior it was impossible to guess the size, the shape or the interior of a house. Until fifty years ago each *mohalla* (neighbourhood) had gates and night-watchmen. A local body known as a *panchayat* kept unwanted persons out of the area with the help of loyal *goondas*. The *panchayats* also arbitrated disputes and managed the *mohalla*. Today the *panchayats*, the watchmen and the gates have disappeared. Life spills out of windows, doors and lanes and seemingly out of every crack and crevice on to Banaras's few major roads. On these roads the traffic is anarchic. They are packed with pedestrians, hawkers, vendors, road-side stalls, hand-carts, bullock carts, horse carriages, rickshaws, packs of donkeys, occasional camels and elephants, wandering cows, scooters, mopeds, three-wheelers, buses and trucks. On these crowded roads I got a feel of the city's 800,000 permanent population and 50,000 floating population.

A less crowded road runs to the British-built Civil Lines. There the houses of the senior civil servants, the law courts, government offices and Westernized hotels are located. From this airy and Anglicized enclave Westernized India is challenging and slowly changing the medieval life lived in the maze of old Banaras lanes.

The citizens of an ageless and ritualistic city like Banaras might be expected to lead a complex life. But on the contrary, the lifestyle of the average Banarasi is simple.

Facing Banaras, across the Ganges, is the great sandbank which draws many Banarasis. They go there to wash, exercise and enjoy themselves in the open, away from the narrow lanes of the crowded city. One of the regular visitors there is Nathu Ram Sardar, a fat and jolly milk seller. I had watched him and his friends row out to the sandbank many times. One day we started talking and I learned that he had recently retired and was supported by his sons, to whom he had left his business. 'I come here every evening,' he explained, 'to have fun with my friends. I like being in the fresh air and having a game of cards after my exercises. Then, in our boat on the river, we grind some *bhang* [cannabis] and condiments to make *thundai* [an aromatic drink]. That is our good life.'

This sense of simplicity and friendliness was common to many of the Banarasis I met: the toy makers, the image makers, the wall painters, the flower sellers, the betel nut sellers, the sweatmeat sellers, the wrestlers, the academics and others. Even some of the rickshaw pullers, whose job is a backbreaking one, spoke with great courtesy and charm. These are the people who attracted me to the city, whose affability balanced the unpleasant behaviour of other Banarasis I had encountered. I was always eager to be invited into their homes and this often happened. Tea was always offered and a chat welcomed.

The truth is that Banarasis are not blasé. They live their lives with a great deal of intensity. Love and hate are common emotions. Indifference is rare. Luckily for me, the acts of kindness outweighed the disagreeable encounters. I shall always remember the betel nut seller near Godowlia who, every time I passed his shop, greeted me with an offering of a scoop of buck-shot-sized betels coated in aromatic silver paper.

In these 2,500 years, Banaras has refined both the seamier and the graceful sides of life. During this time the Banarasis have made it their business to develop and pursue the many pleasures of life. To understand their epicurian nature more fully, I mentioned my meeting with Nathu Ram Sardar to Mahendra Shah, one of the city's aristocrats. 'Do you know *masti*?' he asked, continuing enthusiastically, 'More than *majaa* (fun) and *mauj* (festive enjoyment), *masti* is special to Banaras.'

Masti, he explained, is 'the deep enjoyment of life in which one's inner self is heartily satisfied'. This philosophy of a carefree life (*joie de vivre*) was perfected by Mir Rustom Ali, who governed Banaras after the decline of the Moghul Empire in the early eighteenth century.

To some it may seem that this aspect of the Banarasi lifestyle is decadent. But for the Banarasi, life must be relished to the full. He begins the day with a glass of *thundai* which is often laced with cannabis. Sometimes fine deposits of Ganges silt are also added to it. The morning ablutions are then performed across the river, on the sandbank facing the city. There the sick and the dying do not venture, because it is believed that those who die there will be reborn as asses. The healthy Banarasi washes and dries his clothes on the sandbank, exercises, prays to the seven sacred rivers, anoints himself with sandalwood paste and pats himself with perfumed cotton wisps. These rituals are performed in a leisurely manner, interrupted only by exchanges of views with friends. It is traditional for Banarasis to row out in groups to the sandbank. On the way home, after praying at a temple, they buy curds, sweets and snacks. The midday meal is preceded and followed by a rest. After the afternoon siesta the Banarasi attends to business. If he earns enough to cover that day's expenses he is satisfied. He will close shop or office and resume his *masti*. He is back on the riverbank late in the afternoon and the morning activities are more or less repeated. At dusk prayers are performed at a temple. He then slowly wanders through the bazaar. A connoisseur of *paan*, he must stop at his chosen shop for a chew of betel leaf and betel nut. The preparation of *paan* is a delicate and subtle art in Banaras. Thousands of *paan* makers vie with each other for the artful and tasteful assemblage of the Banarasi *paan* – famous throughout India. Chatting, exchanging greetings and gossip, the Banarasi will then amble towards his favourite *kotha* to be entertained by dancing girls. If he is going home, enroute he will buy *malai*, a rich creamy sweatmeat. *Masti* has variations, particularly with the changing seasons and with the changing times. In today's Banaras few can enjoy the traditional *masti* completely.

Mahendra Shah belongs to one of the wealthy families of Banaras. He relishes the good life. He quit his *havali*, the traditional town house, to live in his garden house near the Sankat Mochan Temple. His mornings are spent playing with his love birds, budgerigars and parrots, or watching the monkeys scamper in the trees near his goldfish tank. Or he may take a stroll in the garden, keeping a watchful eye on the gardener tending his roses. At other times, he may be found reclining languorously on bolsters and cushions in his living room under a chandelier. There he examines his latest purchases: a shawl, a sculpture, a painting, a piece of jewellery. He is a friendly and frequent patron of sculptors, brocade workers, musicians, jewellers and *gulabi meenakari* (pink enamel) craftsmen. In the afternoons he goes to his office in the city, where he supervises the real estate managers who maintain his property. Like most Banarasis, he is addicted to *paan*. At home or in his office, a choice supply is always at hand.

Banaras lies at the crossroads of two ancient arteries of trade: the Grand Trunk Road, the oldest route of north India (a crucial highway even today), and the Ganges, which was a commercial waterway until the railway killed its commerce in the mid-nineteenth century. With the aid of these arteries, the landlords, real estate owners, money lenders, merchants and bankers of Banaras traditionally played an important role in the economic, political, cultural and religious life of the city. Some pre-medieval guilds even maintained armies. Later, during medieval and colonial times, some Banarasis were merchant-bankers to the Moghuls, the Marathas and the British. During British rule, one body of holy men, the Sanyasis, were among the leading merchants of India, trading as far as Bengal and the Deccan Plateau. Their *muths* (monasteries) were channels not only of religion but also of commerce, culture and politics.

Out of the landlord's leisurely lifestyle emerged the *rais* (aristocrat) of Banaras. But the old-style *rais* has disappeared from the city. Modern times preclude the aristocratic patronage of the past. The last of the traditional *rais* was Kishori Raman Prasad, popularly known as Kishori Ramanji. He had a deep passion for music. Of him, Banaras's great *shehnai* (flute) player Bismillah Khan says with a smile and a toss of his hand towards the heavens, 'He was a true *rais*.'

I met Kishori Ramanji when he was seventy-six, two years before his death in 1984. He was short and slim and wore a simple dhoti and shirt all year round. In the winter he would add the long coat-like *angharkha*, or wrap himself in a shawl. His manner reminded me of the actor Chhabi Biswas, who played the music-loving aristocrat in Satyajit Ray's memorable movie, *The Music Room*. Kishori Ramanji showed his appreciation through subtle nuances, like the nod of his head or a small movement of his hand. His son, who has neither the interest nor the means to follow in his father's footsteps, told me: 'Practically every famous musician in India has played in our house and enjoyed our hospitality for weeks, sometimes even for months. After each performance my father would present a purse to the artist.'

On the first anniversary of Kishori Ramanji's death, Ravi Shankar flew to Banaras to perform a special concert in the Raman mansion. Four hundred music lovers, musicians, bureaucrats and pundits attended. Ravi Shankar delighted them with a soulful performance. But these private concerts are rare today, so much so that musicians talk of them with a deep sense of nostalgia. The true connoisseurs and patrons, like Kishori Ramanji, no longer exist. Ravi Shankar's own relationship with Banaras is a poignant example of both the passing of an era and the growing belligerence of Banaras.

Ravi Shankar's performing arts institute sponsors a festival of music every year in the city. In 1986, when I was there, a hall was booked, advertisements were placed in the papers and posters were pasted in the streets. All announced that important artists were to perform. I went with high expectations. Unfortunately, my own feelings were not shared by the Banarasis. The hall was never full. The majority of the audience were young Westerners – travellers, students or short-term residents. Only a sprinkling of Banarasis attended. Even on the final day, when Ravi Shankar played the sitar, though the hall was substantially full, most of the concert-goers were Westerners. The Banarasi connoisseurs were conspicuous by their absence.

But their absence did not seem to affect Ravi Shankar. He poured himself into a mixture of two ragas: *Kamod* and *Kanada*. What did bother him, as he later told a friend, was a pain in his left arm. (Two months later he underwent a heart by-pass operation.) After the intermission he played a duet with his forty-year-old son, whom he introduced with a short speech: 'Friends, this is the first time my son Shuvo Shankar is to play publicly in India. He has performed with me in America. But today I introduce him to India on the sacred soil of Banaras. I seek the blessings of Baba Vishwanathji [Shiva] and you the citizens of our sacred city.'

The concert ended at dawn, but soon he was back in the city with his son to show him the house where he was born and the high school that he attended. This was Shuvo

Shankar's first visit to Banaras. After training as a graphic designer in Bombay, he has lived much of his adult life in the United States.

This trip into the old city revealed Ravi Shankar's feelings for Banaras. His deep ties with the city remain but his relationship with the Banarasis has deteriorated. As he showed me around Hemangana, he remarked: 'I feel I have wasted my money. If I had made the same investment in Delhi, Bombay or Calcutta my efforts would have borne fruit. I had a dream to build an ashram for music. But the response from the Banarasis is not good enough. I do not want money from them, simply appreciation. Under these trees I teach some advanced students every winter but at my music festival, the Banarasis disturb the performances. The town is full of *goondas*. Next year I shall not hold the festival in Banaras. It will be held here in Hemangana. I shall hire buses to transport the guests from the city. At least then I can choose my audience and we can have *majaa*.'

As I walked with the maestro I could see that he has thoughtfully introduced into Hemangana the rural atmosphere of the ashrams of ancient India. The open-air concert space and covered stage is a gesture to modernity. Adjacent to this theater is a double-storied house decorated with lithographs and sculptures of different deities. Ravi Shankar's own prayer and practice room is packed with these images. Here, I watched father and son prepare for their concert. Wisps of smoke floated lazily up from lighted incense sticks. The walls echoed with the sound of the sitar. During pauses in the playing, the muffled roar of traffic from a nearby highway could be heard.

I asked a Banarasi art and music lover, who had trained as a singer in his youth, about the town's attitude towards Ravi Shankar. His response was spontaneous and frank: 'We have the highest regard for Punditji's virtuosity. In spite of his worldwide fame, he has not sacrificed his music on the altar of commercialism. That is an achievement. But we Banarasis want social and intellectual contact with him. He cannot live in an ivory tower. He remains aloof and shuts himself up in Hemangana. He comes here only a few times a year but claims his roots are in Banaras. Look what he has done: he has appointed a *thundai* maker to manage his affairs. We have no truck with such an uncultured man.'

At the music festival, when I enquired about the absence of the cognoscenti, one of Ravi Shankar's men pointed to a man dressed in a Nehru coat and Indian trousers, who sat on a bench outside the auditorium chewing a mouthful of *paan*, and said: 'He is a member of a prominent Banaras family, his forefathers were patrons of music. But look at him; he won't even purchase a ticket for Ravi Shankar's performance. He has come here only to meet Punditji. Why should we give free tickets to such people? Why should he meet Ravi Shankar?'

It then occurred to me that by moving the music festival from the city to Hemangana Ravi Shankar will unwittingly be making the very concession that the music lovers of Banaras demand. The people who shunned his public performances will be invited to his home for private performances. And I wondered who the real prima donna was: the maestro or the Banarasi audience?

Conceit and elitism come naturally to Banarasis, for the city has been India's premier place of learning for 2,500 years. No other city in the world can claim a similar distinction. Seers, scholars and saints have made the pilgrimage to the City of Light in every century of Indian civilization. There are many who have made the pilgrimage to teach, to debate, to seek sanction and to enlarge their knowledge in the ashrams and through their interaction with the pundits of Banaras. Among them, most notably, were the Buddha and Mahavira – the Jain spiritual leader – in the sixth century BC; Patanjali, the Sanskrit grammarian, in the second century BC; Shankara, who laid the foundations of modern Hinduism, in the eighth century; and Ramanuja, the theologian, in the eleventh century.

Today Banaras has several important institutions including a university with a classical Sanskrit name: Varanaseya Sanskrit Vishvavidyalaya, 'The Varanasi Sanskrit Ocean of All Learning'. However, the institution of all-India fame is the Banaras Hindu University, universally known as BHU. It was the brainchild of Madan Mohan Malaviya, the pundit and reformer, who began compaigning for a modern university in 1904. He sought to preserve the best Hindu philosophical and cultural traditions, while maintaining the teaching of modern sciences. He found support among the Theosophists, particularly Annie Besant. It is said that during his tour of India to raise funds, a village woman offered her bangles and a sweeper his day's wages. The Maharaja of Banaras donated 1,300 acres of land and the Viceroy of India, Lord Hardinge, laid the foundation stone in 1916. The campus was arranged in a semicircle, with the administrative buildings in the centre.

Faculties of Sanskrit, Indology, Commerce, Engineering, Agriculture and Medicine were developed. Pundit Madan Mohan Malaviya remained active as the Vice Chancellor until a few years before his death in 1941. The story is told of his refusal to move into Kashi because he did not want liberation, there being much to do in his next lifetime. Ever since its birth and until recently, BHU has been a barometer of the intellectual life of Banaras.

Dr Rai Anand Krishna, the art historian, taught at BHU until his recent retirement. His father singlehandedly assembled the noted art collection of the Bharat Kala Bhavan, BHU's art museum. Dr Anand Krishna believes that BHU is today no longer a part of Banaras. 'It is adrift. The students have cut the umbilical cord which linked BHU to the city's intellectual life. The vibrations which flowed out from here and sparked the city are dead. The BHU of Malaviyaji's vision is no more. Moreover, the intellectuals of Banaras are basking in the glory of the stalwarts of the past like Annie Besant; Bhagwan Das, the modern philosopher; Shiv Prasad Gupta, the philanthropist and visionary, and others.'

The benighted politics of the Gangetic Plain have contributed immensely to the decline of the whole chapatti-flat river belt of Uttar Pradesh State. Along with BHU, other noted universities such as Allahabad University have lost their importance. On a recent visit to BHU I wondered whether there were more armed constables or students. I know of no other university where armed policemen live permanently on the campus. They have been part of the BHU environment since 1972.

Banaras has been a transient city throughout its history. In today's turbulent atmosphere, the decline of the sarangi, a sophisticated musical instrument, symbolized for me the bleak future in store for much of the intellectual and cultural life of the city.

I visited Kabir Chowra, a neighbourhood where musicians have traditionally lived. It is named after Kabir, the legendary fifteenth-century poet. I had an appointment with Pundit Hanuman Prasad Mishra, the last sarangi player of Banaras. His home is located among winding lanes whose *paan*-spattered walls are a free-flowing gallery of a Banarasi version of abstract expressionism.

The sarangi is a string instrument which is played with a bow. It has always been an accompanying instrument. Today's sarangi players are a rare breed. In Banaras, Hanumanji is the last practicing professional. His few students face a bleak future. His two sons, Rajan and Sajan Mishra, are the leading young vocalists in India. They have left Banaras for the public and private patronage of New Delhi. Despite its fate, the sarangi is a remarkable instrument whose sound emulates the human voice better than any other instrument. Its imminent death is due to the rise of the harmonium, an instrument with a curious history. Introduced to India by European missionaries, the harmonium moved from the churches to the nautch halls and brothels and only then found a permanent place as an accompanying instrument in folk and classical music. All India Radio banned the harmonium until 1960 because it does not have the quarter notes and the *midh* or span of Indian music. Moreover, because the harmonium is an easy instrument to play, it was a threat to the sarangi, which is difficult to master. In the department of music at BHU, the sarangi is not even part of the curriculum.

I was ushered into Hanumanji's *baithak*, a living room with green walls on which hung portraits of musicians, including one of his brother the late Gopal Prasad Mishra, a noted sarangi player. A disciple led me to one of the three black plastic sofas. In front of me was a large *masnad* (cushion) on a raised platform a foot high, which covered most of the room. The disciple returned and touched the back of my hand with a swab of cotton dipped in perfume. As a courtesy, I raised my hand to my nostrils to inhale the sweet aromatic *itar*, a perfume with an oil base. At that moment a short, wiry and bespectacled man came in. He was smiling, and his very demeanor suggested the past. He greeted me warmly. Then he began to play Brindabani Sarang, a midday raga. As he ran the bow on the taut sarangi strings the sound was like that of a harsh but beguiling dirge. Hanumanji played for about half an hour until disturbed by a young man loitering in the street below his open window. He stopped and voiced his exasperation with shouts of 'Goonda! Goonda!' The raucous laughter and carefree response filled the room. Hanumanji took off his spectacles and wiped his forehead with his *gamchha*. I found in this scene and in the dirge-like music of the sarangi a metaphor for all the dying art and culture of the Gangetic Plain.

But time has been good to Banaras. The city will survive as it has survived for over 2,500 years. The belief is that Banaras (Kashi) transcends time, and will transcend even the present Age of Strife (Kali Yuga), at the close of which the world will end. Pilgrims will continue to come as they have always done. Holy men will continue to make their presence felt. *Pandas* will continue to pounce on pilgrims. Newly married couples will continue to be blessed by Baba Vishwanath. Childless women will continue to worship the Sun God during the Lolarka Shasthi festival. Widows will continue to seek death in the city of liberation. The dead will continue to be cremated by the Ganges. The devout will continue to worship at the Vishwanath Temple.

Banaras sits on the trident of Shiva, a spiritual manifestation of the Lord of All. It is for this sacred sight that the people of India will always pour into Kashi to seek the inner vision of the unbounded *lingam* of light – the axis of the Hindu universe.

Banaras, May 1987

CAPTIONS

1   *Temples tower over Manikarnika burning ghat, by the Ganges.*

2   *A street shrine to the god Hanuman.*

3   *A half-finished mud sculpture of Bhima, the Son of the Wind, Panchganga Ghat.*

4   *A* panda *(ritual specialist) lounges, and pilgrims prepare for ablutions, Gai (Cow) Ghat.*

5   *On the roof of the house of the Dom Raja, head caretaker of the burning ghats, a woman of the family hangs up washing.*

6   *Banarasis exercise on the sandbank facing the city.*

7   *Swimmers dive from temples half-submerged in the flooded Ganges.*

8   *A man dries his shirt by the Ganges, Darbhanga Ghat.*

9   *A Bengali image maker's son plays with a mask.*

10 *Children play in a lane decorated with wall paintings.*

11 *A woman prays in a Shiva shrine while a goat nibbles flowers, Panchganga Ghat.*

12 *A street cow and clay toys.*

13 *Pall bearers carry a body; the image of the witch Holika is for the Holi festival.*

14 *A priest blesses passersby outside the Vishwanath Temple.*

15 *A beggar and plate and the sculpted guardian of a shrine.*

16 *Musicians lead the funeral procession of a female saint.*

17 *A boy from a tea stall serves customers.*

18 *Moslem women shoppers and their rickshaw driver.*

19 *A bangle seller and customers.*

20 *A street photographer finds customers among pilgrims.*

21 *Banarasis enjoying snacks at a shop.*

22 *A betel-leaf seller and a woman vegetable seller.*

23 *A rickshaw repair shop.*

24 *A milk seller does a tasting in a wholesale milk market.*

25 *Milk sellers, some with bicycles, in the milk market.*

26 *Owner and customers at a betel-nut shop near Godowlia.*

27 *A young assistant of a betel-leaf seller.*

28 *On a rooftop a mother massages her baby.*

29 *A Bengali image maker's wife and daughter in their home.*

30 *A* panda *on his platform attends to pilgrims, Panchganga Ghat.*

31 *Morning worshippers, Panchganga Ghat.*

32 *Pilgrims camp and cook on the eve of a Ganges bath, Dashaswamedh Ghat.*

33 *A man exercises while others wash, swim and perform ablutions.*

34 *Banarasis exercise as their washing dries, Panchganga Ghat.*

35 *Wrestlers and an image of Bhima, one of the protaganists of the* Mahabharata, *Rama Ghat.*

36 *Banarasis after bathing, in front of an image of Ganga (the Ganges).*

37 *Men clean their teeth, a priest prepares to pray, Darbhanga Ghat.*

38 *A barber and client.*

39 *A wrestler holds a* neem *twig for brushing teeth.*

40 *Wrestlers exercise around a Shiva shrine.*

41 *Wrestlers in a pit.*

42 *A café owner takes a nap.*

43 *An Indian club painted with the image of a cow.*

44 *The winner of an Indian club competition.*

45 and 46 *Imaginative tableaux during Nakkatiya festival, part of the* Ramayana.

47 *Children play with sparklers during Diwali, the festival of lights.*

48 *A man places lighted candles on his rickshaw, Diwali Festival.*

49 *Banarasis celebrating Holi, the spring harvest festival.*

50 *Holi revellers in front of an erotic wall drawing.*

51 *In a street performance, a snake charmer and opponent cast spells on each other by means of* mantras *(magic words).*

52 *Street singers and musicians entertaining passersby.*

53 *Rooftop make-up for staging the epic* Ramayana.

54 *The Maharaja of Banaras's retainers before the start of a Dusserah Festival procession.*

55 *Lolarka Shasthi, a fertility festival honouring the Sun God (left).*

56 *A father and two sons at the Lolarka Shasthi.*

57 *A priest and clients and an image of the Sun God.*

58 *A pilgrim crowd camps near the Lolarka sacred tank.*

59 *Staging of Bharat Milap, a climactic part of the* Ramayana.

60 *A Banarasi performing morning exercises.*

61 *A pilgrim prays at a tree-shrine, Gai Ghat.*

62 *A Moslem graveyard.*

63 *A goat in a Banaras lane.*

64 *Retainers at the Maharaja of Vijainagram's Banaras Palace.*

65 *Banaras* rais *(aristocrat) Mahendra Shah's wife and daughter in their living room.*

66 *The Maharaja of Banaras Vibhuti Narain Singh and his daughter and grandson, Dusserah Festival, at Ramnagar Fort.*

67 *Pundit Hanuman Prasad Mishra plays the sarangi at home.*

68 *Ravi Shankar and son Shuvo Shankar embrace after a sitar concert.*

THE PLATES

1

3

4

9

11

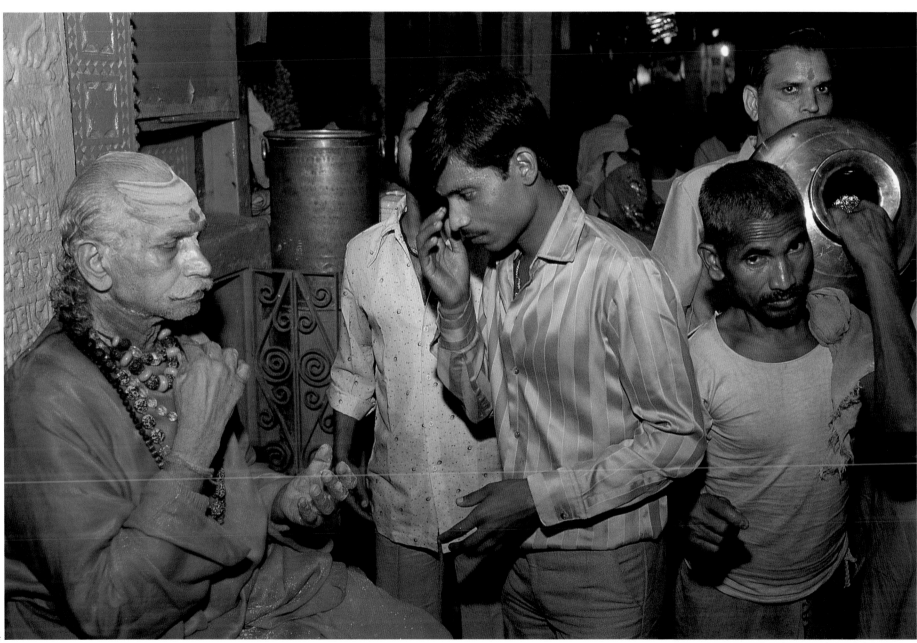

23

24

27

28

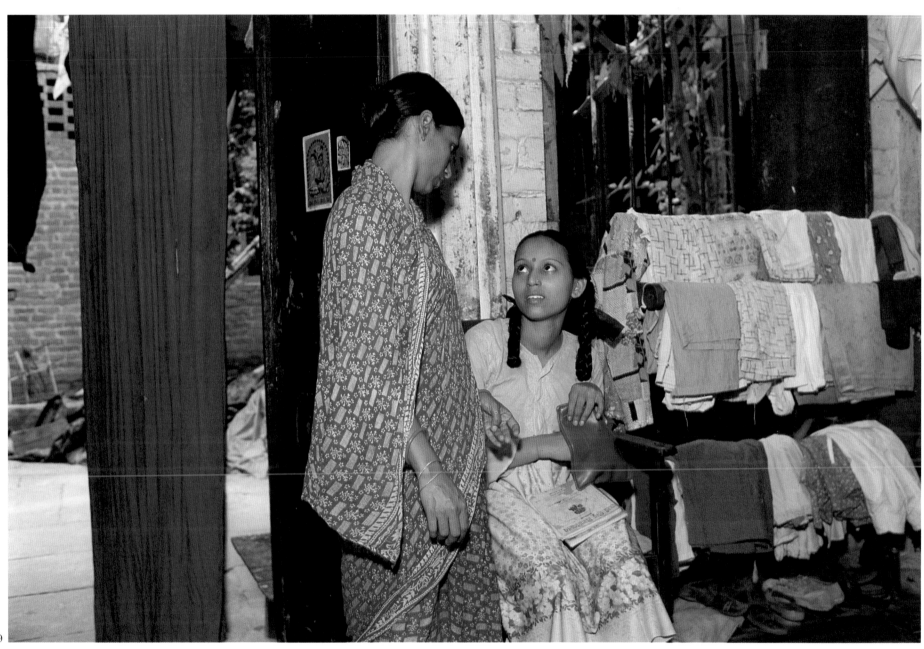

35

46

54

60

61

63

79

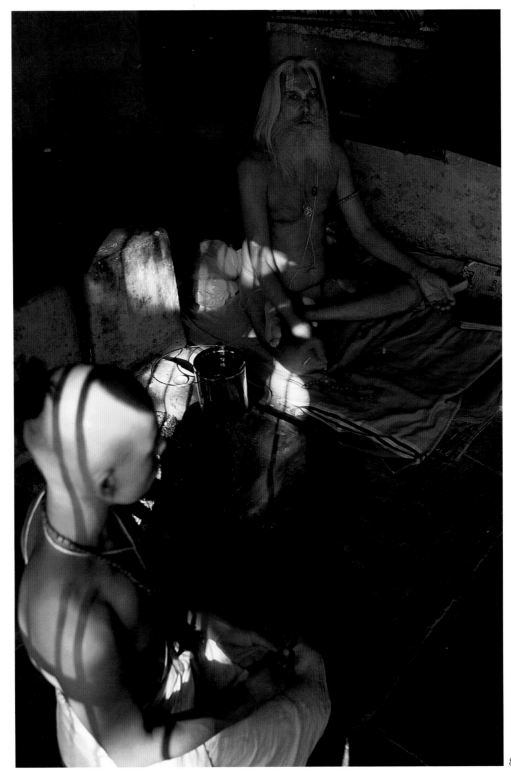

85

89

91